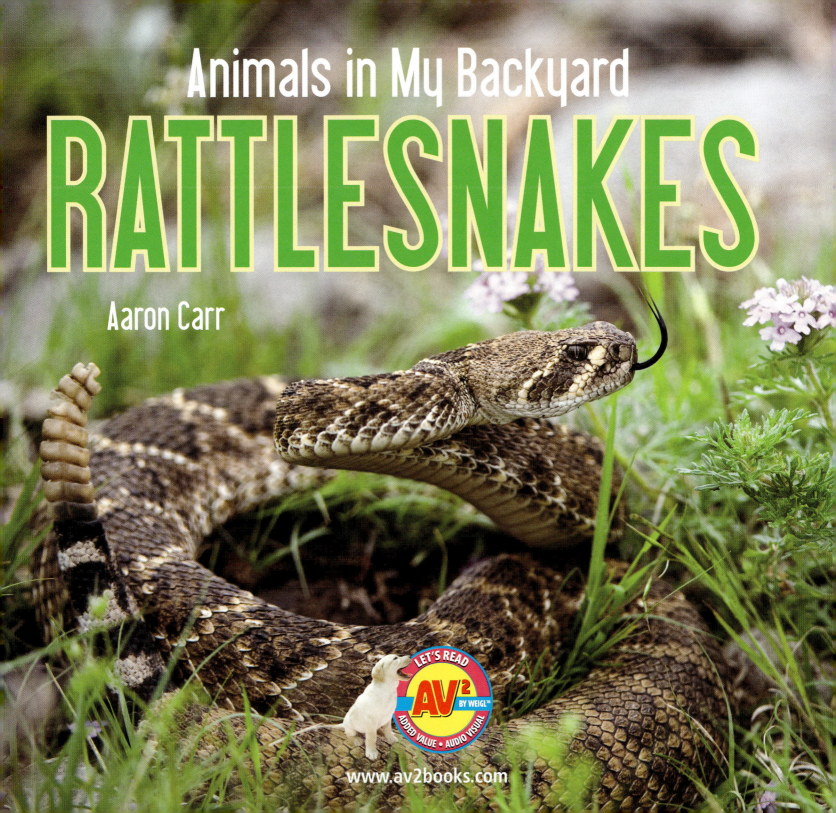

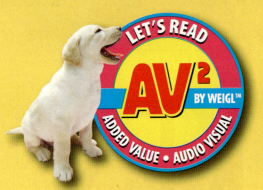

AV² provides enriched content that supplements and complements this book. Weigl's AV² books strive to create inspired learning and engage young minds in a total learning experience.

Your AV² Media Enhanced books come alive with...

 Audio
Listen to sections of the book read aloud.

 Key Words
Study vocabulary, and complete a matching word activity.

 Video
Watch informative video clips.

 Quizzes
Test your knowledge.

 Embedded Weblinks
Gain additional information for research.

 Slide Show
View images and captions, and prepare a presentation.

Try This!
Complete activities and hands-on experiments.

... and much, much more!

Go to www.av2books.com, and enter this book's unique code.

BOOK CODE

U762857

AV² by Weigl brings you media enhanced books that support active learning.

Published by AV² by Weigl
350 5th Avenue, 59th Floor New York, NY 10118
Websites: www.av2books.com   www.weigl.com

Copyright ©2015 AV² by Weigl
All rights reserved. No part of this publication may be reproduced, stored in a retrieval system, or transmitted in any form or by any means, electronic, mechanical, photocopying, recording, or otherwise, without the prior written permission of the publisher.

Library of Congress Control Number: 2013953034

ISBN 978-1-4896-0548-1 (hardcover)
ISBN 978-1-4896-0549-8 (softcover)
ISBN 978-1-4896-0550-4 (single-user eBook)
ISBN 978-1-4896-0551-1 (multi-user eBook)

Printed in the United States of America in North Mankato, Minnesota
1 2 3 4 5 6 7 8 9 0 17 16 15 14 13

122013
WEP301113

Project Coordinator: Aaron Carr   Designer: Mandy Christiansen

Weigl acknowledges Getty Images as the primary image supplier for this title.

Animals in My Backyard
RATTLESNAKES

CONTENTS
- 2 AV² Book Code
- 4 Meet the Rattlesnake
- 6 Family
- 8 Rattling Tail
- 10 Large Fangs
- 12 How He Smells
- 14 How He Sees
- 16 How He Stays Warm
- 18 Where He Lives
- 20 Safety
- 22 Rattlesnake Facts
- 24 Key Words

Meet the rattlesnake.

He is a large snake.

When he was young,
he lived with his mother.

He lived with his mother for two weeks before going off to live on his own.

He has a rattle on the end of his tail.

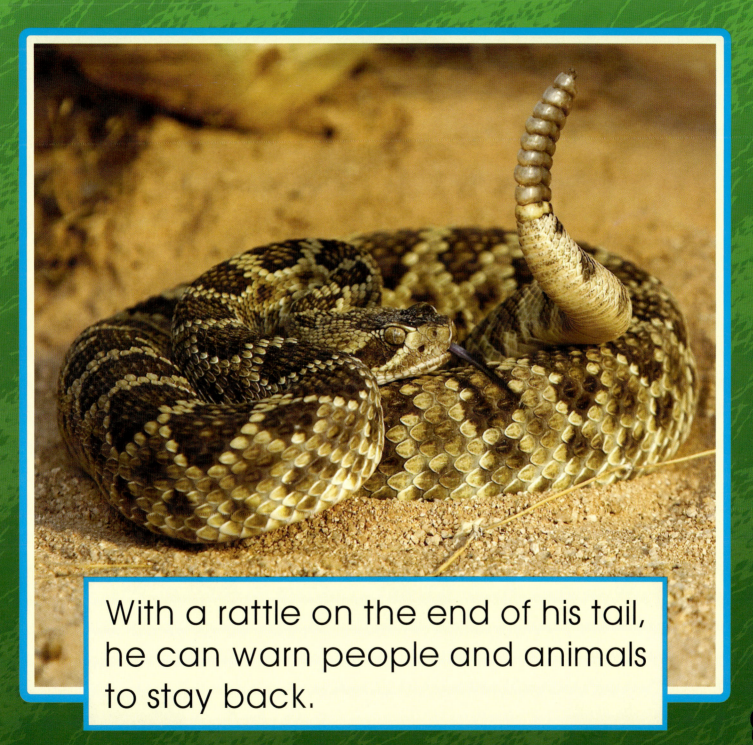

With a rattle on the end of his tail, he can warn people and animals to stay back.

He has two big fangs.

His two big fangs
keep him safe from other animals.

He smells by using his tongue.

Using his tongue helps him smell if other animals are close.

He can see other animals in the dark.

In the dark, he can see heat coming off an animal's body.

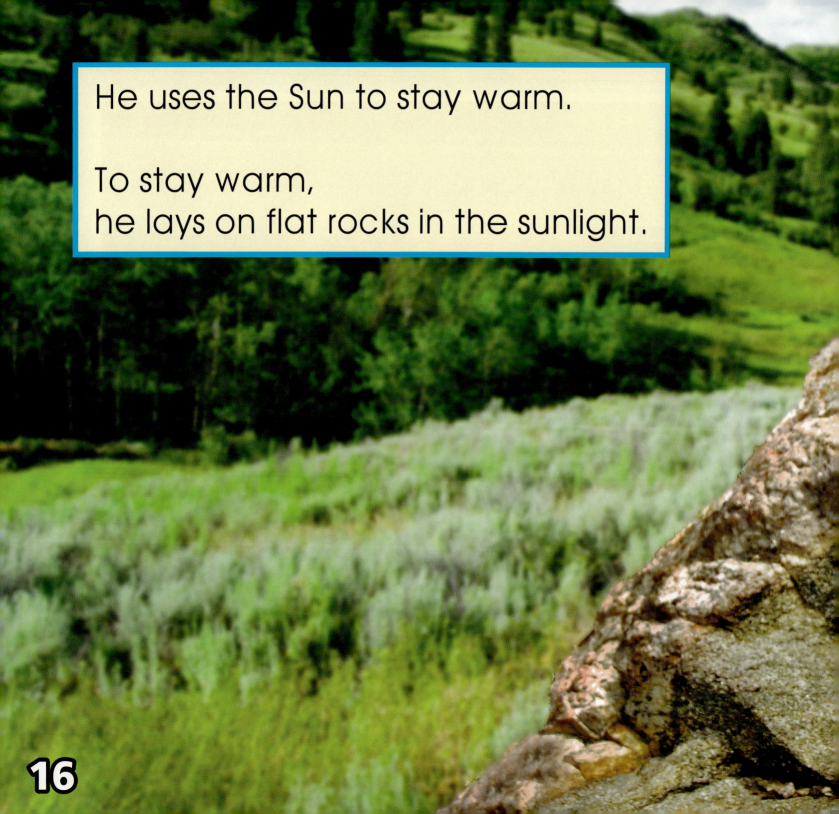

He uses the Sun to stay warm.

To stay warm,
he lays on flat rocks in the sunlight.

He lives in a hole in the ground.

This hole in the ground is called a den.

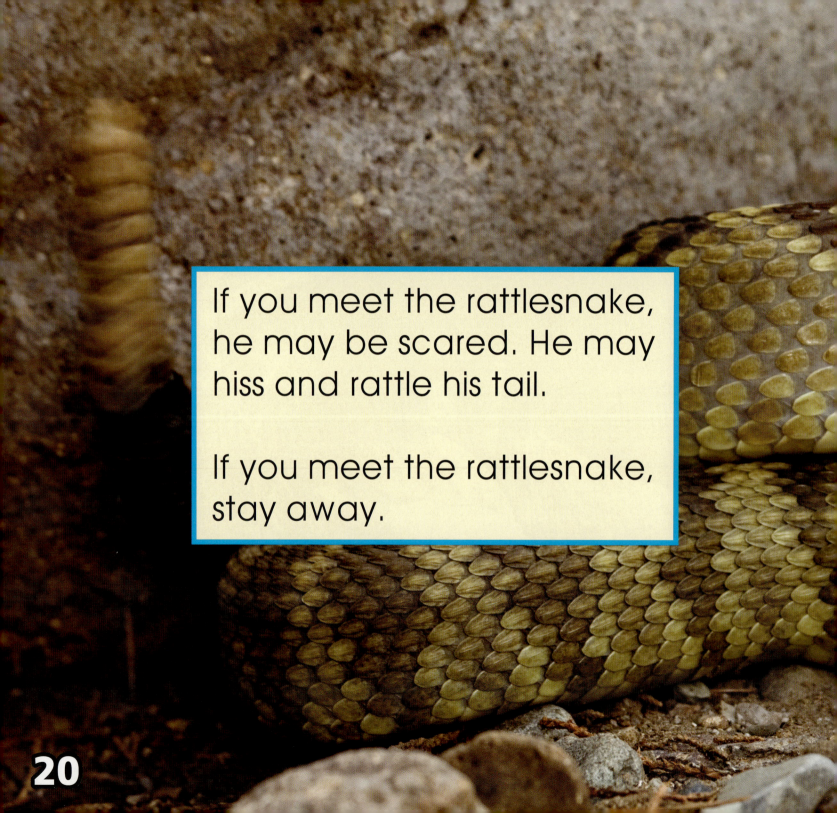

If you meet the rattlesnake, he may be scared. He may hiss and rattle his tail.

If you meet the rattlesnake, stay away.

RATTLESNAKE FACTS

These pages provide more detail about the interesting facts found in the book. They are intended to be used by adults as a learning support to help young readers round out their knowledge of each animal featured in the *Animals in My Backyard* series.

Pages 4–5

Rattlesnakes are large snakes. There are 33 rattlesnake species in the pit viper family. Most rattlesnakes are between 1.6 and 6.6 feet (0.5 and 2 meters) long, but they can be more than 8 feet (2.5 m) long. Rattlesnakes can be identified by their distinctive tails and color patterns. Most rattlesnakes have patterns of diamonds or hexagons on their backs. These patterns are most often in shades of gray or brown.

Pages 6–7

Rattlesnakes live with their mothers when they are young. Unlike other reptiles, rattlesnakes do not lay eggs. Females carry the eggs inside them for about 90 days. The baby is born in a clear, soft wrapper. Once outside of its mother, the baby tears through the wrapper. Baby rattlesnakes stay with the mother for two weeks. After this, they molt, or shed their skin, for the first time and go off on their own.

Pages 8–9

Rattlesnakes have rattles on their tails. They are born with a knob on the end of the tail, called a pre-button. The first ring forms with the rattlesnake's first molt, but it cannot make the rattling sound until at least two rings have formed. New rings are added with each molt, but older rings break off regularly. The rings are made of keratin. This is the same material fingernails are made of.

Pages 10–11

Rattlesnakes have two large fangs. These teeth are hollow, which allows the rattlesnake to inject venom when it bites. It only takes one-fifth of a second for a rattlesnake to inject venom into its prey. This venom is very strong and can kill animals many times larger than the rattlesnake. Rattlesnakes only eat when they are hungry. This means they may go up to two weeks without eating.

Pages 12–13

Rattlesnakes use their tongues to help them smell. They have a tongue that forks into two points. The rattlesnake flicks its tongue up and down quickly to help it pick up smells in the air. The rattlesnake has a Jacobson's organ on the roof of its mouth. This organ works like a nose to help the rattlesnake smell.

Pages 14–15

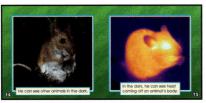

Rattlesnakes can see in the dark. They have a type of heat vision that lets them "see" the heat other animals give off. Like all pit vipers, the rattlesnake has heat sensitive pits on each side of its head. Signals from these pits are sent to the same part of the rattlesnake's brain that processes signals from the eyes. This allows the rattlesnake to hunt in complete darkness.

Pages 16–17

Rattlesnakes use the Sun to keep warm. Like all reptiles, rattlesnakes are cold blooded. This means they do not make their own body heat. Instead, rattlesnakes must rely on the Sun to keep them warm. When rattlesnakes get cold, they lay in sunlight to warm up. If they become too hot, they crawl into underground burrows to cool down.

Pages 18–19

Rattlesnakes live in holes in the ground. Depending on the species and habitat, rattlesnakes may live in holes in the ground, in rock crevices, or under piles of leaves. In cold climates, rattlesnakes hibernate through the winter in underground dens. They gather in dens in large numbers. Hundreds of rattlesnakes of different species may hibernate in the same den.

Pages 20–21

If you meet the rattlesnake, stay back. Rattlesnakes usually stay away from people. They do not attack unless they feel threatened. If a person surprises a rattlesnake, though, it may become scared and defensive. It shows this by coiling its body, raising and shaking its rattle, and hissing. Rattlesnake bites are deadly enough to kill people. However, effective cures for rattlesnake venom are widely available.

KEY WORDS

Research has shown that as much as 65 percent of all written material published in English is made up of 300 words. These 300 words cannot be taught using pictures or learned by sounding them out. They must be recognized by sight. This book contains 47 common sight words to help young readers improve their reading fluency and comprehension. This book also teaches young readers several important content words. These words are paired with pictures to aid in learning and improve understanding.

Page	Sight Words First Appearance
4	the
5	a, he, is, large
6	before, for, his, lived, mother, off, on, own, to, two, was, when, with, young
8	end, has, of
9	and, animals, back, can, people
10	big, two
11	from, him, keep, other
12	by
13	are, close, helps, if
14	in, see
15	an
16	uses
19	this
20	away, be, may, you

Page	Content Words First Appearance
4	rattlesnake
5	snake
6	weeks
8	rattle, tail
10	fangs
12	tongue
14	dark
15	body, heat
16	rocks, Sun
18	ground, hole
19	den

Check out www.av2books.com for activities, videos, audio clips, and more!

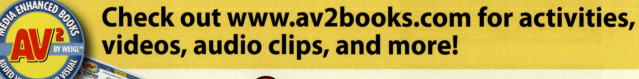 Go to www.av2books.com.

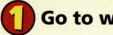 Enter book code. U 7 6 2 8 5 7

 Fuel your imagination online!

www.av2books.com